BEYOND THE BATTLEFIELD

Code Makers & Code Breakers

ALLEN R. WELLS

Twice big group = Battalion

...ght group = Squad

...shooting gun = Mach...

Rourke
Educational Media

A Division of
Carson Dellosa Education

Before Reading: *Building Background Knowledge and Vocabulary*
Building background knowledge can help children process new information and build upon what they already know. Before reading a book, it is important to tap into what children already know about the topic. This will help them develop their vocabulary and increase their reading comprehension.

Questions and Activities to Build Background Knowledge:
1. Look at the front cover of the book and read the title. What do you think this book will be about?
2. What do you already know about this topic?
3. Take a book walk and skim the pages. Look at the table of contents, photographs, captions, and bold words. Did these text features give you any information or predictions about what you will read in this book?

Vocabulary: *Vocabulary Is Key to Reading Comprehension*
Use the following directions to prompt a conversation about each word.
- Read the vocabulary words.
- What comes to mind when you see each word?
- What do you think each word means?

Vocabulary Words:
- Allies
- codes
- cryptanalysis
- digital data
- radiotelegraph
- secure

During Reading: *Reading for Meaning and Understanding*
To achieve deep comprehension of a book, children are encouraged to use close reading strategies. During reading, it is important to have children stop and make connections. These connections result in deeper analysis and understanding of a book.

Close Reading a Text
During reading, have children stop and talk about the following:
- Any confusing parts
- Any unknown words
- Text to text, text to self, text to world connections
- The main idea in each chapter or heading

Encourage children to use context clues to determine the meaning of any unknown words. These strategies will help children learn to analyze the text more thoroughly as they read.

When you are finished reading this book, turn to the next-to-last page for **After-Reading Questions** and an **Activity**.

Table of Contents

Code Makers
Choctaw Code Talkers

In 1918, during World War I, the United States Army had a communication problem. The quickest way to relay important information was by phone. But the Germans tapped phone lines and could listen in on messages. The United States tried creating **codes**, but the Germans kept cracking the codes, revealing American secrets.

codes (kohdz): systems of words, letters, symbols, or numbers used instead of ordinary words to send messages or store information with the goal of keeping the messages and information secret

One day, two soldiers were talking together in a camp. These two soldiers were Choctaw people, an American Indian group. An army captain walked by them and overheard their conversation. They spoke in a language he didn't recognize. He asked what language they were speaking. The soldiers told him it was Choctaw. That gave the captain an idea!

A group of Choctaw code talkers pose for a photograph.

CONFIDENTIAL

Right away, a specialized squad of Choctaw soldiers was formed to send coded messages for the army. Many American Indian groups have their own languages. These languages are not widely known by people outside of the groups. Most were also not written down. Because of this, the Choctaw language made the perfect secret code.

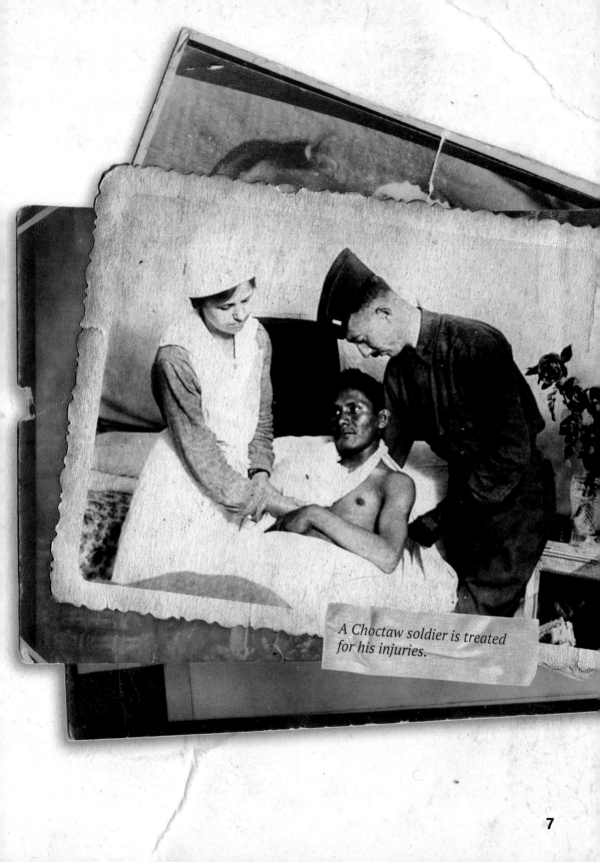

A Choctaw soldier is treated for his injuries.

This group of Choctaw soldiers came to be called the Choctaw code talkers. They were placed in strategic locations so they could relay important information between each other. The Choctaw soldiers even created a code within the Choctaw language, so they used a code within a code.

Choctaw Language in the U.S.

Though the Choctaw language was key in creating an unbreakable secret code, it was not viewed as valuable across the U.S. Choctaw children, along with other American Indian children, were punished for speaking anything other than English in schools. The U.S. government was using the Choctaw language to their advantage, while at the same time trying to get rid of it.

The Germans were still listening in, but they had no idea what the Choctaw soldiers were saying. This was one code they would never crack.

Twice big group = Battalion

Eight group = Squad

Fast shooting gun = Machine gun

Additional secret codes were used for common military words in order to create a code within the Choctaw language. For example, instead of saying "Battalion" in Choctaw they would say "Twice big group."

Navajo Code Talkers

The Choctaw code talkers led the way for the Navajo code talkers. During World War II, the U.S. Marine Corps looked to the Navajo people to create another unbreakable code.

They started out with 29 Navajo people who volunteered to be code talkers. These volunteers created a code based on their unwritten Navajo language. This language was particularly difficult to understand, even compared to Choctaw. Once the code was created, a code talking school was formed in 1942. There other Navajo people were trained to be code talkers.

The orignal 29 Navajo code talkers are sworn in as members of the U.S. Marine Corps.

The Navajo code talkers were part of many important marine battles during WWII. They were often put in groups of two. One code talker would be stationed at the battle site. The other would be stationed near headquarters. The code talker in battle would send important information, communicate strategy, and ask for supplies and ammunition when they ran low.

Navajo code talkers

Around 420 Navajo people served as code talkers by the end of WWII. They were known as being fast and accurate when delivering messages. They contributed to multiple U.S. victories during WWII. Their code is the only code used by the U.S. Army that has never been cracked.

A group of Navajo code talkers pose for a photograph.

The Green Hornet

The U.S. was pulled into WWII after Japan attacked the Pearl Harbor naval base in Oahu, Hawaii, in 1941. Shortly before this tragic event, American code breakers decoded a message from Japan. The message said Japan was no longer looking to settle problems with the U.S.

General George Marshall was given this information and knew it could mean war. He wanted to let those stationed in the Pacific know there could be a threat because they were closest to Japan. This included Hawaii. The problem was, General Marshall didn't have a **secure** way to alert Pearl Harbor. The Germans, who were Japan's allies, were listening in on phone calls.

Instead, Marshall sent the message by **radiotelegraph**, which took more time to deliver than a telephone call. By the time his warning arrived, the attack on Pearl Harbor had already happened.

A ship explodes during the Pearl Harbor attack.

secure (si-KYOOR): safe from danger

radiotelegraph (RAY-dee-oh TEL-i-graf): a device that sends messages over long distances using a code of electrical signals by radio waves

In 1942, Bell Telephone Laboratories was hired by the U.S. Army to create a way to communicate securely over the phone. That's when they came up with a device that could turn speech into **digital data**. The coded speech was then communicated over the phone and was unbreakable by an enemy. If someone tried listening in, all they would hear is a buzzing sound. It got the nickname "the Green Hornet" after the show of the same name. The buzzing sound resembled the show's theme tune. Over time, it came to be called SIGSALY.

Speech is translated into digital data and can only be deciphered with a key in the SIGSALY system.

Hello! %≈¤Ӡ√? Hello!

digital data (DIJ-i-tuhl DAY-tuh): information represented with a machine language system

SIGSALY was put into use all over the world. It solved the issue of unsecured communications. It was particularly important for communication between U.S. President Franklin Delano Roosevelt and United Kingdom (U.K.) Prime Minister, Winston Churchill. The Germans could no longer listen in, and these important leaders could communicate securely.

This mock-up of SIGSALY is on display at the National Cryptologic Museum. It only shows one third of the system; the whole thing weighed 110,000 pounds (49,895.2 kilograms)!

CODE BREAKERS

Alan Turing

During WWII, the Germans were using a machine called Enigma to send encoded messages to their military. It is thought that this machine could create around 159 quintillion different code arrangements. Because of this, the Germans believed their machine was an unbreakable code creator.

Alan Turing joined the U.K.'s Bletchley Park code-breaking team when they declared war on Germany in 1939. Turing's ideas were key to the team's success. They created a device called the Bombe that was able to crack the codes of Germany's Enigma.

The German code-creating machine, Enigma

Alan Turing

The Bletchley Park code-breaking team

19

The Bombe brought military information to the **Allies** for the remainder of the war. After the war was over, the British government named Turing an Officer of the Most Excellent Order of the British Empire for his work decoding Enigma. Turing and his team are now credited with helping to end the war.

Turing's Legacy

Turing is not only remembered for his contributions to WWII, but also for his contributions to the field of computer science. His ideas were some of the foundations of technology behind today's computers, laptops, and smartphones. He also laid the groundwork for the beginnings of artificial intelligence.

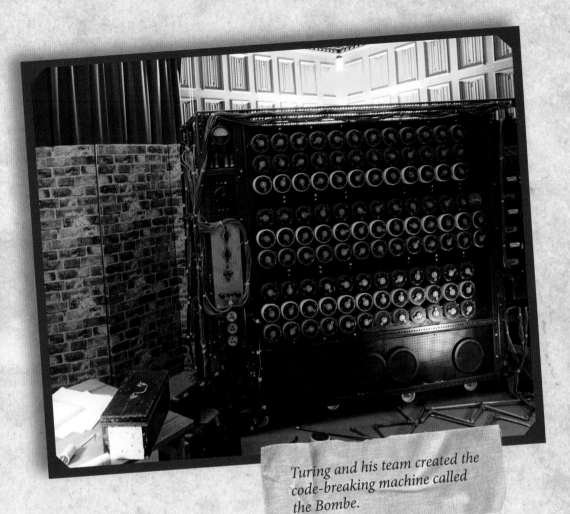

Turing and his team created the code-breaking machine called the Bombe.

Allies (AL-eyez): the group of nations, including the United States, Britain, the Soviet Union, France, and China, that fought against the Axis powers (Germany, Italy, and Japan) during WWII

Despite all Turing did for the war and science in general, he was labeled a criminal at the time of his death. Turing was in a relationship with a man named Arnold Murray, but homosexuality was a criminal offense at this time. When their relationship was discovered, Turing pled guilty in court. He was punished cruelly as a result.

Turing died by apparent suicide two years later. In 2009, British Prime Minister Gordon Brown issued a public apology on the government's behalf for the treatment of Turing. Now, the Bank of England's 50-pound note will feature an image of Turing. Today, he is remembered for his incredible contributions to science.

Bank of England

m-config.	Symbol	Operations	Final m-config.	
q_i	S_j	PS_k, L	q_m	
q_i	S_j	PS_k, R	q_m	(N_1)
q_i	S_j	PS_k	q_m	(N_2)
				(N_3)

$q_1 S_0 S_1 R q_2$; $q_2 S_0 S_0 R q_3$; $q_3 S_0 S_2 R q_4$; $q_4 S_0 S_0 R q_1$;

Fifty Pounds

"This is only a foretaste of what... and only the shad...

Alan Turing

A statue of Alan Turing in a park in Manchester, England.

ALAN TURING
CODE BREAKER & PIONEER OF COMPUTER SCIENCE
LOVE LIVED HERE
1912-1954

Code Girls

During WWII, U.S. federal agencies started recruiting people to become code breakers. With so many men already at war, they turned to women. Women were not expected to have careers during this time period, so it was a surprising move. From college graduates to schoolteachers, women across the U.S. were contacted to join this **cryptanalysis** division.

The work was hard. They were packed into crowded offices during the hot summer. They worked 12-hour days, 7 days a week. They knew if they made a mistake it could put someone's life in danger.

cryptanalysis (KRIP-tuh-NAL-i-sis): the solving of a coded communication system

Arlington Hall was one of the buildings transformed into a workspace for these code breakers.

The information these women gathered allowed troops to sink enemy ships, bring down enemy planes, and plan other attacks. Near the end of the war, these code breakers provided so much information on Japanese supply ships that the military couldn't keep up and sink them all. This slow but steady sinking of enemy supplies was a huge part of the Allies' success in WWII.

An enemy ship sinks during WWII.

One of these code breakers, Virginia D. Aderholt, was the first American to find out the war was over. Germany had already surrendered when a message from Japan was intercepted. Aderholt decoded the message and it contained Japan's surrender.

When the war ended, many women returned to the lives they led before the war. But a few stayed on. Most notably was Ann Caracristi, who became the first woman to hold the position of deputy director of the National Security Agency (NSA).

Ann Caracristi

The efforts of the women involved in code breaking during the war were unknown for decades. Their work was kept secret and they were asked to stay quiet for years. This was in the interest of national security. While it is uncertain exactly how many of these women contributed to the war as code breakers, historians believe there were at least 10,000.

Two code-breaking veterans, Nancy Tipton (left) and Katherine Fleming, talk to one another at a reunion put on by the Veterans History Project.

Memory Game

Look at the pictures. What do you remember reading on the pages where each image appeared?

Index

After-Reading Questions

1. Why did the Choctaw language make a code that was difficult to crack?

2. What is one characteristic the Navajo code talkers were known for?

3. Why was SIGSALY needed?

4. What was the name of the device Turing helped create to crack Enigma's code?

5. What is the name of the first woman to be deputy director of the National Security Agency?

Activity

Think about the different types of codes you read about in this book. Write down at least two to compare. List some of the advantages of each code. Then, list a potential disadvantage. If you were going to choose one of the codes you read about to communicate a secret message, which would you choose?

About the Author

Allen R. Wells loved researching and refamiliarizing himself with the hidden figures in this book. Allen admires their perseverance and determination to fight for what they believe. He writes wherever he finds inspiration. He lives in Atlanta, Georgia, where he works as a mechanical engineer and children's author.

www.rourkeeducationalmedia.com

PHOTO CREDITS: cover: eastern archive/ Shutterstock.com, LiliGraphie/ Shutterstock.com, Leonsbox/ Getty Images, SergeKa/ Getty Images, Wicki58/ Getty Images, FabrikaSimf/ Shutterstock.com; Inside Cover: DarkBird/ Shutterstock.com, Leonsbox/ Getty Images, SergeKa/ Getty Images, Wicki58/ Getty Images; TOC: waku/ Shutterstock.com; TOC, page 32: TADDEUS/ Shutterstock.com; page 4, 10, 14, 18, 24: DarkBird/ Shutterstock.com; page 4-6, 6-7, 14-15, 26-30: DarkBird/ Shutterstock.com page 5, 7, 9, 11-12,13, 15-16, 17, 19, 21, 23, 25, 26, 28-29: Picsfive/ Shutterstock.com; page 5, 30: Oklahoma Hisotrical Society; page 5: Tolga TEZCAN/ Getty Images, DNY59/ Getty Images; page 6: Morphart Creation/ Shutterstock.com, FabrikaSimf/ Shutterstock.com, Leonsbox/ Getty Images; page 7: Wikimedia Commons, DarkBird/ Shutterstock.com; page 8, 20: LiliGraphie/ Shutterstock.com; page 8: ParkerDeen/ Getty Images, Brand X Pictures/ Getty Images, page 9: SergeKa/ Getty Images, Wicki58/ Getty Images; page 10, 20: DarkBird/ Shutterstock.com; page 11: U.S. National Archives and Records Administration, DarkBird/ Shutterstock.com; page 12-13, 22-23, 28-29: sozon/ Shutterstock.com; page 12, 30: National Archives Catalog; page 12 YuniqueB/ Shutterstock.com; page 13: National Archives, Records of the U.S. Marine Corps; page 15: Everett Collection/ Shutterstock.com, Ivan Smuk/ Shutterstock.com; page 16-17: photonova/ Shutterstock.com; page 16: FabrikaSimf/ Shutterstock.com; page 17: Wikimedia Commons; page 18-19: Olga_Z/ Getty Images; page 19: BMCL/ Shutterstock.com, Wikimedia Commons; page 19, 30: by kind permission, Director GCHQ, courtesy Bletchley Park Trust, Nataliia K/ Shutterstock.com; page 20: Wikimedia Commons, Ulza/ Shutterstock.com; page 21: EQRoy/ Shutterstock.com; page 23: amirraizat/ Shutterstock.com, Wikimedia Commons; page 23, 30: Bank of England; page 25: Wikimedia Commons, Tolga TEZCAN/ Getty Images, US Government courtesy of the National Cryptologic Museum, ESB Professional/ Shutterstock.com; page 26, 30: Wikimedia Commons, Nataliia K/ Shutterstock.com; page 27: US Government courtesy of the National Cryptologic Museum, Merydolla/ Shutterstock.com; Milos Luzanin/ Shutterstock.com; page 28, 30: Wikimedia Commons; page 29: Shawn Miller, Library of Congress, Twin Design/ Shutterstock.com

Edited by: Hailey Scragg
Cover and interior design by: Morgan Burnside

Library of Congress PCN Data
Code Makers and Code Breakers / Allen R. Wells
(Beyond the Battlefield)
  ISBN 978-1-73164-903-4 (hard cover)
  ISBN 978-1-73164-851-8 (soft cover)
  ISBN 978-1-73164-955-3 (e-Book)
  ISBN 978-1-73165-007-8 (ePub)
Library of Congress Control Number: 2021935274

Rourke Educational Media
Printed in the United States of America
01-1872111937